SPORTING 🏆 HEROES

GREG RUTHERFORD

ROY APPS

ILLUSTRATED BY ALESSANDRO VALDRIGHI

HIGH LIFE HIGHLAND	
3800 17 0032741 8	
Askews & Holts	03-Jan-2018
B RUT	£8.99

Franklin Watts
First published in Great Britain in 2017
by The Watts Publishing Group

Text © Roy Apps 2017
Illustrations © Watts Publishing Group 2017
Illustrator: Alessandro Valdrighi
Cover design: Peter Scoulding
Executive Editor: Adrian Cole

*The statistics in this book were correct at the time
of printing, but because of the nature of the sport,
it cannot be guaranteed that they are now accurate.*

HB ISBN 978 1 4451 5334 6
PB ISBN 978 1 4451 5337 7
Library ebook ISBN 978 1 4451 5335 3

1 3 5 7 9 10 8 6 4 2

Printed in China

Franklin Watts
An imprint of
Hachette Children's Group
Part of The Watts Publishing Group
Carmelite House
50 Victoria Embankment
London EC4Y 0DZ

An Hachette UK Company
www.hachette.co.uk

www.franklinwatts.co.uk

2002, MILTON KEYNES ATHLETICS CLUB.

Y-E-E-S-S, JOEY! GOOD RUN!

SOME OF THE CLUB'S YOUNG ATHLETES ARE SHOWING THEIR SKILLS TO A GROUP OF VISITORS.

NOW, WATCH THIS YOUNG LONG JUMPER.

WHEN YOU SEE HIM ON THE TV IN YEARS TO COME, REMEMBER THAT YOU FIRST SAW GREG RUTHERFORD TRAINING HERE.

GET YOURSELF HOME AND HAVE AN EARLY NIGHT, GREG. YOU'RE JUMPING IN AN EVENT TOMORROW, DON'T FORGET.

YEAH, RIGHT.

CHAPTER TWO
NOT SO LONG JUMP

Greg was sixteen when athletics coach Tom McNab invited him to join an elite group of promising young athletes in his home town of Milton Keynes. Joining the group didn't come cheap — it cost £200 a month — but somehow Greg's parents found the money, even though they weren't well off.

Greg still had his taste for late nights, clubbing and fast cars, though.

In the summer of 2004, when he was seventeen, Greg won the long jump Amateur Athletic Association Under 20 Championship with a jump of 7.24 metres.

'Didn't I say you had real talent?' Tom McNab told him.

The win meant that Greg could compete for Great Britain in their next international match against Australia.

The venue was in Manchester. There was a real buzz about the place. All the country's best young athletes were on show. Greg was particularly excited: it was the first time he had worn a Great Britain vest.

As the track events got underway, Greg's fellow British athletes began taking first and second places. Greg was the British Under 20 Long Jump Champion, could he get a first place result here?

'And next is Greg Rutherford, for Great Britain...'

Greg finished seventh out of a field of eight.

A few days later, Greg was sitting in a car with his mates. They were trying to cheer him up.

CHAPTER THREE

SUPERKID!

6th July 2005: the elite athletes group had been training hard when Tom McNab called them over.

'Let's go upstairs to the canteen. There's something on TV we all need to watch.'

On the TV the International Olympic Committee were about to announce which city had won the right to host the 2012 Olympic Games.

'The International Olympic Committee has the honour of announcing that the Games of the 30th Olympiad in 2012 are awarded to the city of… LONDON!'

Greg turned all his energies to training.

At the 2005 European Junior Championships in Lithuania he jumped 8.14 metres; the first time he had broken through 8 metres. That jump was a new British Junior record.

The following year, Greg became the youngest member of the GB senior athletics team. He went on to win a silver medal at the European Championships in Sweden.

That success led to him being noticed by the press, and appearing in national newspapers.

For the first time in his short career, Greg began to believe that he was on his way to the top.

CHAPTER FOUR
DON'T MENTION THE DOGS!

Winning European Silver should have been the start of something big for Greg; instead it was the start of everything falling apart.

Greg had already parted company with his coach, Tom McNab, whose monthly fee had doubled to £400. Greg's parents couldn't afford that sort of money.

On top of that, Greg kept missing events because he was ill or injured.

'If it's not my hamstrings, it's my ankle,' he told his friends. 'And I keep kept getting throat infections!'

'At least you have a job,' they told him.

Greg chuckled. 'UK Athletics told me I have to get a flat in London, so I can train with my new coach at Brunel University. The only money I get is £10,800 National Lottery funding. From this I pay for everything: rent, food, clothes, sports kit and travel,' he said.

Greg thought his new coach, Frank Attoh, was almost as bad as his parents, he was that strict.

'Nothing must get in the way of your progress as an athlete, OK? So no girlfriends — and definitely no pets!' Frank said.

Greg didn't tell Frank, but he had bought two Labrador puppies. As they grew bigger, they became his regular training partners. He took them on runs through the woods and hills near his home; something he knew that Frank wouldn't agree with.

'How are your two lovely Labs?' one of his training partners asked him.

Suddenly, Greg saw Frank approaching.

'Shhh!' he replied. 'Don't mention the dogs! Not in front of Frank!'

Running through the woods with his Labradors, Dexter and Murphy, Greg started to think:

'Why am I doing this? I had enough of being poor as a kid. I don't want to be a poor adult. And if I'm always injured, how will I ever get anywhere?'

When he got home, he went online. He found out about joining the Royal Air Force and the police.

He told his best mate, 400-metre runner Andrew Steele, that he was thinking about other jobs he could do…

CHAPTER FIVE
THE SADDEST TIME

One day, early in 2008, Greg called in at home after spending an afternoon training in Milton Keynes. He found his mum in the kitchen. She was crying.

'Mum? What is it?'

'It's your Grandad Jim,' she said, between sobs. 'The hospital tests aren't good. He hasn't got long to live.'

Greg's world fell apart. His grandad Jim had always been someone special to him. Jim had been a gifted sportsman, and had once been signed to Arsenal FC. Greg had always believed that he had inherited his sporting talent from his Grandad Jim.

In the world of athletics, everyone was gearing up for the 2008 Olympic Games in Beijing. Greg divided his time between training and visiting his grandad in hospital.

Just before he was due to fly out to Team GB's training camp in Macau, Greg's grandad died.

'I need a few more days at home. So that I can go to Jim's funeral,' he told his coach.

'Greg, you're preparing for the Olympics now. You must know that any days you miss training will affect your performance,' his coach replied.

So Greg boarded the plane with the rest of the team. But he hated the fact that he'd not been able to say a proper goodbye to his grandad. It was the saddest time.

When it came to the long jump final in Beijing's National 'Bird's Nest' Stadium, Greg tried to spur himself on by thinking of Grandad Jim. But something was wrong.

Greg felt emotionally drained after losing his grandad. But it wasn't that, and he wasn't injured either. Something just felt wrong with his body.

He defaulted on two jumps. His third was just 7.84 metres. He ended up 10th.

Straight after the event, the rep from Nike, who sponsored him, was furious.

'Make sure that never happens again,' he snarled, and stormed off.

Back in his room, Greg collapsed.

Later, his room-mates couldn't wake him up. They called the team doctor.

The doctor took one look at Greg, then turned to his room-mates, a deadly serious expression on his face.

'He needs to get to hospital, quickly!'

CHAPTER SIX
NEW CAR, NEW COACH...?

At the hospital, the doctors found that Greg was seriously ill. He had tonsillitis, bronchitis and a serious kidney infection.

But despite his illness and his disappointing performance in Beijing, Greg was still a professional athlete. Once he was back home, he was asked to represent Team GB at a special lunch hosted by SportsAid, an organisation that helps young British athletes financially.

The day didn't start well. On the way, Greg's old car developed a nasty rattling sound. Greg wondered was wrong with it, until there was an almighty bang and the exhaust fell off.

Greg arrived at the lunch late and a bit grubby from trying to fix the exhaust. The event was full of smart-suited business people and city types. Greg felt very out of place.

One of the businessmen walked over to him.

'Greg, isn't it? I'm Ian Bullerwell.' He shook Greg's rather grimy hand. 'I run a business not far from where you live. We'd be interested in sponsoring you — you're one of our local young sporting heroes.'

After his embarrassment in Beijing, Greg couldn't have felt less like a sporting hero, but who was he to argue with a potential sponsor?

'Thanks. Yes, I'd be very interested.'

Ian Bullerwell's sponsorship meant that Greg was able to buy a decent car: a Saab 93. He also had his warm-weather training and flights to athletics events paid for.

Greg's sponsorship was a great boost for him. Things still weren't quite right, though. He wasn't jumping as well as he needed to if he was going to be in with a chance of a medal at the London Olympics. He knew what the problem was. He just wasn't happy with his coach.

Then, in November 2009 came the following announcement:

'American Dan Pfaff to become new UK Athletics Guru!' Greg knew all about Dan Pfaff. He was one of the most respected coaches in the world, and had worked with four-time Olympic long jump gold medallist Carl Lewis.

'But would he be interested in coaching me?' Greg wondered. 'I've never won anything on an international level. Would he think I've got the potential? Well, there's only one way to find out. I'll just have to ask him.'

CHAPTER SEVEN
AGONY

Greg met Dan Pfaff and told him of his dreams and ambitions for London 2012.

'Uh-huh,' said Dan.

'Well?' asked Greg. 'Would you consider becoming my coach?'

'Uh-huh.'

'Yeah?'

'Sure.'

'That's great!' Greg was excited — and relieved.

Right from the start Greg hit it off with Dan Pfaff. Unlike Greg's previous coach, he didn't just shout out instructions, but took time to explain why the different training drills were important.

There was still one thing Greg hadn't mentioned to Dan, though: his dogs. Eventually, he realised he'd have to bring the subject up.

'Dan, what do think about athletes owning pets, like dogs?'

'Well, if you like dogs, that's fine, isn't it?'

'You see, I've got these two Labs who go hill sprinting with me—'

'Fine. If it works for you.'

So, Greg carried on running through the woods with Dexter and Murphy; only now he didn't have to worry about his coach finding out.

The training continued to go well. In August 2010, Greg set a new British long jump record of 8.35m. Later that year, he won Silver in the Commonwealth Games in Delhi, India.

Everything was coming together very nicely in time for the 2012 London Olympic Games.

At the beginning of 2012, the Team GB athletes flew out to South Africa for warm-weather training. The practice jumps were going well. Greg felt on top form. He thundered down the track, pushed out his leg ready to take off, then,

'Aargh!'

Greg crashed to the ground in agony. His hamstring had torn.

Greg was devastated. For almost seven years, his dream had been to compete at the London Olympic Games. Now, he sat on the track, hardly able to stand, his dream shattered.

CHAPTER EIGHT
GOLD

After months of specialist physiotherapy, Greg was able to start jumping again. In July, just 27 days before the Olympic qualifying round, Greg pulled his hamstring again.

For two weeks he sat in a hyperbaric chamber in a London hospital, breathing in oxygen through a face mask. A hyperbaric chamber works by pumping higher levels of oxygen around the body, improving the chances of injuries healing quickly.

At the end of the two weeks, Greg was feeling fit. He flew out to Portugal with other British athletes to take part in the final preparations for the Olympic Games.

In London, as he walked out of the tunnel with Team GB, the roar of the crowd was deafening. Greg knew that everyone there was willing the British

athletes to succeed. Could he do it?
Could he win an Olympic medal?

Greg got through the qualifying rounds
in fourth place.

Saturday 5th August 2012: 80,000 people filled the Olympic Stadium. The cheer that went up as Greg begun his run-up for the first jump was so ear-shatteringly loud, that for a brief moment he was put off his stride. He mistimed his jump and only just cleared 6 metres.

As he returned to the runway for his second jump, the stadium suddenly went quiet. Greg heard a voice shout out into the silence,

'C'mon, Greg! This is your time!'

The roar of the crowd started to grow once more, but this time Greg didn't hear it. He just powered down the track and jumped: 8.21 metres. He was in the lead.

In the third jump, he fouled, but in the fourth jump he leapt 8.31 metres, more

than enough to keep top spot and take
the gold medal.

A little later, Greg stood breathless on
the podium, gold medal around his neck.
He was smiling at the cheering crowd.

When he stepped down, he was
surrounded by reporters.

After becoming Olympic champion, Greg's success continued. In 2014, he jumped 8.51 metres, a new British record.

In the same year he won a Commonwealth Games gold medal.

At the World Championships in 2015 he won gold again, this time with a jump of 8.41 metres, his second longest jump ever.

In 2016, he defended his European Championship title and took bronze at the Rio Olympics.

Greg was honoured in his home town of Milton Keynes with a giant 8-metre tall metal statue. It's called, what else... 'Leaping Man'.

SPORTING 🏆 HEROES

FACT FILE

Full name: Gregory James Rutherford

Date of birth: 17th November 1986

Place of birth: Milton Keynes, UK

Height: 1.88m (6ft 2in)

Club: Marshall Milton Keynes Athletics Club

GLOSSARY

bouncer — a person employed by a club or pub
to keep out troublemakers or underage customers

defaulted — in long jump, to step over the takeoff board line and
recieve a red flag, so the jump doesn't count

elite — the most highly skilled

hamstrings — tendons (strong fibres) at the back of the knee

inherit — to have something passed down from older generations
of the same family

press — used to describe journalists from the news media

sponsorship — to give or receive money in return for promoting
or advertising a product or company

warm-weather training — when athletes travel to a warm
location to continue outdoor training during the winter

CAREER

Key Medals:
Men's long jump

European Junior Championships, gold medal	2005
European Championships, silver medal	2006
Commonwealth Games, silver medal	2010
Olympic Games, gold medal	2012
Commonwealth Games, gold medal	2014
European Championships, gold medal	2014
World Championships, gold medal	2015
Olympic Games, bronze medal	2016
European Championships, gold medal	2016

Other Achievements:
• Greg was appointed MBE (Most Excellent Order of the British Empire) by the Queen in 2013.

Mel sat with Adam and his parents at home in their sitting room.

'If Adam's going to make it to the top — and he's got the talent — it'll mean big changes for you all.'

'How do you mean?' asked Adam's dad.

'Adam's going to have to get up early for a start. By early I mean 4.30am,' added Mel.

Adam's jaw dropped. 'Half past four! Are you serious?'

CONTINUE READING
ADAM PEATY'S
AMAZING STORY IN ...